Ed Sheeran

By Rachel Seigel

CRABTREE
PUBLISHING COMPANY
WWW.CRABTREEBOOKS.COM

RAP 3 2401 00917 873 4

CRABTREE
PUBLISHING COMPANY
WWW.CRABTREEBOOKS.COM

Author: Rachel Seigel

Editor: Kathy Middleton

Photo research Crystal Sikkens, Ken Wright

Proofreader: Lorna Notsch

Design and prepress: Ken Wright

Print coordinator: Katherine Berti

Photo Credits

Alamy: pp 16, 18-19, WENN Ltd; p 21 (top), sjvinyl; p 23, Jada Images; pp 24, 26, PA Images / Alamy Stock Photo; p 28, Storms Media Group / Alamy Stock

AP Images: p 10, STEPHEN HIRD;

Getty: p 8, Cindy Ord; p 15, Matt Jelonek; p 14, Kirk McKoy; p 17, Michael Kovac; p 20, Mark Venema; p 21 (bottom), Christie Goodwin; p 22, JOHN STILLWELL; p 25, David M. Benett; p 27, Alex B. Huckle

Keystone: front cover, Keystone Press via ZUMA Press

Shutterstock title page, Randy Miramontez; p 5, JStone; p 6, Twocoms; p 7, Featureflash Photo Agency; p 9 (right). Keith Homan; p 11, Andrea Raffin; p 12, yakub88; pp 14-15 (bkgd), maziarz

Wikimedia: p 4, Mark Kent

Library and Archives Canada Cataloguing in Publication

Seigel, Rachel, author
        Ed Sheeran / Rachel Seigel.

(Superstars!)
Includes index.
Issued in print and electronic formats.
ISBN 978-0-7787-4832-8 (hardcover).--
ISBN 978-0-7787-4847-2 (softcover).--
ISBN 978-1-4271-2095-3 (HTML)

        1. Sheeran, Ed, 1991- --Juvenile literature. 2. Singers-
-England--Biography--Juvenile literature. I. Title. II. Series:
Superstars! (St. Catharines, Ont.)

ML3930.S54S45 2018   j782.42164092   C2018-900277-8
                                                                        C2018-900278-6

Library of Congress Cataloging-in-Publication Data
Names: Seigel, Rachel, author.
Title: Ed Sheeran / Rachel Seigel.
Description: New York, New York : Crabtree Publishing
        Company, 2018. | Series: Superstars! | Includes index.
Identifiers: LCCN 2018005819 (print) |
        LCCN 2018006382 (ebook) |
        ISBN 9781427120953 (Electronic) |
        ISBN 9780778748328 (hardcover) |
        ISBN 9780778748472 (pbk.)
Subjects: LCSH: Sheeran, Ed, 1991---Juvenile literature. |
        Singers--England--Biography--Juvenile literature.
Classification: LCC ML3930.S484 (ebook) |
        LCC ML3930.S484 S45 2018 (print) |
        DDC 782.42164092 [B] --dc23
LC record available at https://lccn.loc.gov/2018005819

Crabtree Publishing Company

Printed in the U.S.A./052018/BG20180327

www.crabtreebooks.com   1-800-387-7650

Published in Canada
Crabtree Publishing
616 Welland Ave.
St. Catharines, ON
L2M 5V6

Published in the United States
Crabtree Publishing
PMB 59051
350 Fifth Avenue, 59th Floor
New York, New York 10118

Published in the United Kingdom
Crabtree Publishing
Maritime House
Basin Road North, Hove
BN41 1WR

Published in Australia
Crabtree Publishing
3 Charles Street
Coburg North
VIC 3058

CONTENTS

Words that are defined in the glossary are in
bold type the first time they appear in the text.

All Eyes on Ed

Ed Sheeran is a British pop singer-songwriter known for such hit singles as "Thinking Out Loud" and "Photograph." He blends many different styles of music into his songs, such as folk, hip-hop, dance, soul, and rock. He classifies his overall sound as "acoustic soul with hip-hop influences." His musical influences range from folk/pop singer Bob Dylan to rapper Eminem. Irish folk music has also had an influence on his music. He often listened to this style of music when he visited his Irish grandparents.

Many of Ed's songs are about things that have happened in his life, such as love, heartbreak, growing up, and becoming famous.

Finding Success

Ed's first single hit number one on the iTunes chart before he ever signed with a record label. He has sold millions of records, had more than 150 nominations, and won 76 awards for his music. He has performed at the closing ceremonies for the 2012 London Summer Olympics, and had a song appear in the movie *The Hobbit: The Desolation of Smaug.*

A Rapping Ginger

Ed Sheeran's red hair and casual style of dressing are his trademarks. When he was younger, he believed his hair made him stand out. Now he knows his red hair makes him **unique**. He is known for having a sweet nature and for being **humble**. He has never forgotten how much he struggled in the past, and says that being famous is a "blessing" that he can never take for granted.

Be Happy!

Ed is grateful to his fans—who are known as "Sheerios"—for accepting him for who he is. In return, he hopes to inspire and reassure them to be happy with who they are.

Working Hard

Ed believes that he is successful because he believed in himself, worked hard, and never gave up. When he was a kid, his father gave him an article about a singer named James Morrison. It stated that Morrison performed more than 200 gigs a year to get experience before signing with a label. That article inspired Ed. He knew where he wanted to be one day, and that the way to get there was through the amount of hard work he was willing to put in.

A singer and songwriter from England, James Morrison got his start by playing his guitar on the streets as a teenager.

They Said It

"25 Times Ed Sheeran Really Was the Nicest and Hardest Working Guy in the Industry."
—E! News. February 16, 2016

Growing Up

Edward Christopher Sheeran was born on February 17, 1991, in Halifax, England. When he was young, his parents John and Imogen moved him and his older brother Matthew to Suffolk, where he spent the remainder of his childhood. As a child, he was known by the nickname "Teddy," but now he prefers to be called Ed. Growing up, Ed often felt he didn't fit in. He was born missing an eardrum in one ear, wore big,

thick glasses, and spoke with a **stutter**, which is thought to have been caused by the removal of a large birthmark on his face.

Around age nine, his dad bought him a copy of Eminem's album *The Marshall Mathers*, and by the time he was 10, he had learned all the lyrics to the songs. Emimem raps very fast and very carefully, and copying him made Ed's stutter almost disappear. He says he still stutters occasionally when he gets excited.

In 2015, Ed was honored at the American Institute for Stuttering's Freeing Voices Changing Lives Benefit Gala where he gave a speech about stuttering.

Artistic Upbringing

Ed grew up in an artistic and creative household. His parents loved art and were involved in organizing important art exhibitions around the world. His mother later went on to become a jewelry maker. Many of her handmade jewelry pieces were created to help local charities. His brother Matthew studied music at college, and is now an award-winning classical music composer.

Ed's Jewelry

Imogen Sheeran created a collection of jewelry inspired by Ed. The jewelry pieces are based on such things as his favorite candies and his song lyrics.

Many of Imogen's jewelry pieces feature foods, such as licorice allsorts, smarties chocolate candies, and even cans of soup and beans!

Campbell's CONDENSED Chicken Noodle SOUP

Campbell's CONDENSED Tomato SOUP

Starting Points

Ed and his brother grew up in a fairly strict household. His parents limited the amount of TV they were allowed to watch and banned video games. Instead, they bought them lots of art books. Before deciding to become a singer, Ed thought he might like to be a painter. He even sent early paintings to a kids' show called *Blue Peter*.

Ed believes the starting point for his love of song came at age four, when he sang with his mother in the church choir. His parents didn't like rock music, but were fans of such artists as Bob Dylan, Eric Clapton, and Joni Mitchell. They often listened to these musicians when the family traveled to London for business. Ed quickly learned the words to their songs and began singing along. All the music featured acoustic guitar, and it made an impression on him.

Ed picked up his first guitar after he saw Eric Clapton perform the song "Layla" at Queen Elizabeth's Golden **Jubilee** in 2002.

Starting Points

As Ed's love for music began to take over, his schoolwork suffered. He wasn't an ideal student, but his teachers recognized his musical potential. He credits his music teacher as being one of his inspirations.

Another major musical inspiration of Ed's was Irish folk singer-songwriter Damien Rice. Ed saw Damien perform at Whelan's, a club in Ireland, when he was 11 years old. After the concert, he was able to meet Damien. Ed says the time he spent talking with him was inspiring. After the meeting, he went straight home and started writing songs.

Damien Rice

He Said It

"... when I saw Damien play at Whelan's, [it] literally changed my life. The time he spent talking with me after the show made all the difference. It inspired me in a way that I only hope to do for someone else."
—capitalfm.com, January 19, 2015

Finding His Spark

Ed believes the more songs you write, the better a songwriter you become. He has said that he uses songwriting as a way to make himself feel better when he's having a bad day. He tries to write as much as possible. When he's preparing an album, he can write as many as four to five songs a day. The perfect song for him is something that makes the listener feel the emotions described in the lyrics.

Ed received his first guitar as a gift from his uncle. He learned to play it on his own before taking actual music lessons.

He Said It

"I think any time I've ever got down or ever felt low, the one thing that picks me up from that is writing a song about it because at least you've got a positive experience out of a bad experience."
—Interview on BBC Radio Four's *Desert Island Discs* May 7, 2017

Making Music

When Ed Sheeran was 11, he performed his first "gig" in front of his classmates. At first he was afraid to go onstage, but he overcame his fear and performed Eric Clapton's hit song "Layla." As his musical confidence grew, he started performing his own songs. He often performed at school concerts and family weddings.

At age 13, Ed recorded his first collection of songs, or EP, titled *The Orange Room*. The recording featured five tracks, some of which were from his **demo**. Thinking he could find more gigs in the city, he headed to London for the summer at age 14, with only his guitar, a looper pedal, and a backpack full of clothes.

Looper pedals record music and play it back to you, so you can record another line over top of it. Since Ed performs alone, a looper pedal helps him copy the sound of a band.

Chasing His Dream

In 2007, Ed was accepted into the Youth Music Theatre UK in London. This experience helped Ed advance his musical career by giving him the confidence to perform in front of large crowds. The following year, he left high school and moved to London permanently to **pursue** his music.

While in London, Ed spent a few years sleeping on friends' couches. If he couldn't find a couch, he'd sleep on the train. This experience inspired his song "Homeless."

YMT

The Youth Music Theatre UK provides education and opportunities for young people ages 11–21 to act and perform in new musical theater productions.

Getting Gigs

Ed played as many gigs as he could while he was in London. He played gigs in small venues, and sold CDs out of his backpack to make some extra money. He sometimes performed to groups as small as five people. There were even times when only his parents were there. In 2008, he played more than 300 gigs. By the time he got a real paying gig, he had played over 400 gigs for free. Every experience added to his next show. He learned how to be more polished, and how to perform and interact with fans.

Once, Ed even slept outside Buckingham Palace, where Queen Elizabeth and her family live.

Building Buzz

Ed learned early on how to use the Internet to help boost his career. He **promoted** his gigs on social media, and started getting the attention of many new followers. The Internet not only helped Ed gain attention from fans, but also the notice of a rapper named Example, who asked him to go on tour with him as his opening act. This experience gave him more exposure and helped open the door to future opportunities.

Ed Sheeran has 20.4 million followers on Twitter and 15.3 million on Instagram.

American Adventure

Early in 2010, Ed decided to drop everything and go to Los Angeles. His plan was to stay a month and share his music with as many people as he could. He decided to leave some of his music at a radio station where actor/singer Jamie Foxx was hosting a radio show. Jamie liked what he heard and invited Ed to an open mic night he was putting together. When Ed first came onstage, the audience was a little unsure about him, but Ed won them over and soon they were on their feet cheering.

Ed stayed with his friend, actor Jamie Foxx, for six weeks while trying to launch his career in Los Angeles.

Making It

Ed's experiences throughout 2010 helped inspire him to write and release three collections of songs that year. In January 2011, he released his fifth and final collection of songs as an independent artist. The EP, entitled *Number 5* **Collaborations** *Project*, rose to number two on the iTunes chart without any promotion. It sold more than 7,000 copies in its first week and gained the attention of Atlantic Records, which later offered him a recording contract, and Elton John who signed him to his management team.

66 He Said It 99

"I was a hard sell for the major labels. Here's a ginger kid who raps with a guitar. That's not a good start."
—*Mail Online* February 11, 2012

Breaking Through

Soon after, Ed started preparing his first album. He promoted it by releasing two singles, "The A Team" and "You Need Me, I Don't Need You" in the summer of 2011. The singles both reached the Top 10 on the UK Singles Chart and created positive media attention for his upcoming album. Finally, on September 9, 2011, Ed's first studio album + (Plus) was released in Ireland. It was released in other countries throughout the following year, ending with the US in June 2012.

LEGO House

Ed's third single off his + album was "LEGO House," which referenced his favorite toy, LEGO. He asks for a small LEGO set at each of his stops when he is on tour to help him relax. He sometimes even throws LEGO pieces into the crowd.

Ed is seen here performing songs from + (Plus) at HMV in Dublin, Ireland, in September 2011.

On the International Stage

The album + was an instant success. It sold more than one million copies in the UK in its first six months. Soon after its release, Ed went on the road, touring the UK and North America to promote the album. He quickly became an international sensation and gained countless fans around the world.

Ed's Ink

Ed has more than 60 tattoos. Each of them has a special meaning. They represent things in his life that are important to him, such as his family, achievements, milestones, and memories.

When his album + (Plus) reached number one in the UK, Ed celebrated by having a plus symbol tattooed on his left wrist.

Topping the Charts

In June 2014, Ed released his second album, *X* (Mutiply). Now, with a worldwide fan base, it is no surprise that this new album peaked at number one in 15 countries. It was both the best and fastest-selling album in the UK that year. Three years later, Ed continued his math theme and released his third album, ÷ (Divide), in March 2017. This album broke a record, with 56.7 million listens in 24 hours, and has passed one billion views on YouTube.

While on tour to promote his *X* album, Ed played three sold-out shows at Wembley Stadium in London. The shows became part of a documentary entitled *Jumpers for Goalposts: Live at Wembley Stadium*.

21

Recognition and Rewards

The success of Ed's music has earned him a number of awards and achievements over the years. He has won close to 80 awards, including an American Music Award, three People's Choice Awards, and four Grammy Awards. His latest Grammy Awards received in 2018, were for Best Pop Solo Performance for his song "Shape of You" and Best Pop Vocal Album for his album ÷.

A special achievement for Ed came in December 2017, when he was awarded an MBE (Member of the Order of the British Empire) by Prince Charles. This honor was given to him for his services to music and charity.

Royal Recognition

Receiving his medal in 2017 wasn't the first time Ed has been recognized by the British royal family. He also performed at the Queen's Diamond Jubilee in May 2012. There were 20,000 people in the audience, including a special area for members of the royal family and VIPs. There were 250,000 members of the public outside the arena, and the TV audience was worldwide. Before the show, Ed tweeted to his fans: "So apparently 1 billion people are tuning in tonight. No pressure then." After the performance, he tweeted, "Well that was fun."

He Said It

"It was an honor to play the Queen's Jubilee and such an honor to be part of that lineup."
–David Nolan, *Ed Sheeran: A+ The Unauthorized Biography*, 2014

Touring with Taylor

Ed Sheeran has been lucky to tour with many popular musicians, including Taylor Swift. Taylor invited Ed to open for her North American Red tour in 2013. Since then, they have become close friends. He even wrote and recorded a song with her called "Everything Has Changed." During each stop of Taylor's Red tour, Ed would join her onstage to sing this duet together.

Famous Friends

Aside from Taylor Swift, Ed has worked with many famous musicians. He has written songs for such artists as Christina Aguilera, One Direction, and The Weeknd. In 2017, Ed recorded two remixes of his song "Perfect." One was with his friend Beyonce, and the other was with Andrea Bocelli.

Sheeran says one of his biggest moments was meeting his idol, guitarist Eric Clapton. Over time, the two became friends, and Ed even sang on one of Eric's records. Eric then returned the favor by recording music on Ed's album ÷.

Justin Bieber can thank Ed for providing him with his hit song "Love Yourself." Ed had originally wrote that song for himself, but later decided not to use it. He said it was a better fit for Justin.

Doing Good

Giving is something Ed Sheeran is known for. He says he keeps enough money to be comfortable, and the rest goes to family, friends, and charity. He is passionate about helping people in need and supports many charities relating to AIDS and HIV, children, creative arts, health, and poverty. In early 2017, Ed participated in "Red Nose Day," which is a yearly event that raises money to end child poverty. He traveled to Liberia to meet with homeless and parentless children. He was so moved by one boy's story that he rescued him and four of his friends and arranged for them to get proper shelter and education.

Ed Sheeran gave his time to the Teenage Cancer Trust series of charity gigs at the Royal Albert Hall in London.

❝ He Said It ❞

"Ed Sheeran's Attitude to Money Will Make You Wish You Were His Mate (friend)."
– Jenny Mensah, Radio X, March 14, 2017

Gingerbread Man Records

Ed has also found a way to **mentor** other struggling musicians. In 2015, he set up his own record label, called Gingerbread Man Records. With Ed's help, talented artists have the chance to promote their music over the radio, on the Internet, or in live performances. He has recently set up a YouTube channel for Gingerbread Man Records that features music videos from his newly signed artists.

British singer and songwriter Jamie Lawson was the first person to be signed to Gingerbread Man Records.

What's Next?

Ed Sheeran rose to fame quickly. As grateful as he is for the success of his career, his sudden fame also took a toll on him. Before the release of his newest album ÷ *Divide*, he took a year off to focus on himself and battle a problem he was having with **substance abuse**. He said it was his love of music and his girlfriend Cherry Seaborn that helped him overcome this dark time in his life.

Ed is now looking to the future. He has recently asked Cherry to marry him and hopes to start a family in the coming years. He will continue touring the world to promote his album ÷ into 2019. Fans might even see him on the big screen in the near future, as he is in talks to develop a musical film starring himself and his music. If that's not enough, Ed's followers can always look forward to the release of his fourth album, rumored to be called *Subtract*, which will complete his mathematical series. As far as the future goes, Ed has said he has achieved more than he ever thought he could, so whatever comes next for this talented ginger will be icing on the cake!

Cherry Seaborn is an English hockey player. She and Ed met in high school and started dating in 2015.

Timeline

1991: Edward Christopher Sheeran is born on February 7 in Halifax, England

2004: Begins recording music and releases his first collection of work called *Spinning Man*

2007: Accepted into Youth Music Theatre UK in London

2008: **Auditions** for the TV series *Britannia High* but doesn't get the part

2009: Studies music at the Academy of Contemporary Music

2010: Posts his first video online and is invited to tour with the rapper Example

2011: Ed reaches Number two on the iTunes Chart for *Number 5 Collaborations Project*

2011: Releases his first studio album + (Plus), which debuts at number one on the UK Albums Chart

2012: Wins Brit Award for Best British Male Solo Artist and British Breakthrough Act of the Year

2012: Performs at the Queen's Diamond Jubilee

2013: Nominated for a Grammy award for Song of the Year

2013: Opens for Taylor Swift in her Red tour

2014: Releases new album X in May

2014: Sets out on first world tour

2015: Sets up his own music label Gingerbread Man Records

2016: Takes a break from music and social media

2017: Releases two singles, "Castle on the Hill" and "Shape of You," from new album ÷

2017: Releases "River" with Eminem

2017: Sets out on Divide world tour

2018–2019 Becomes first artist in UK history to have three different albums stay in the top 10 of the UK album chart for at least one year

Glossary

audition An interview for a musical or theatrical production, where candidates demonstrate their performance abilities

collaboration Something worked on together with another person

demo Short for demonstration, a recording of a performer to showcase their talent to a company

jubilee A jubilee is a special anniversary celebration. The Queen's Golden Jubilee celebrated 50 years being queen. Her Diamond Jubilee celebrated 60 years as queen.

humble To be modest

mentor An adviser or teacher

promote To encourage interest in something

pursue To try to accomplish something

stutter To speak in an uneven way with uncontrolled repeating or interruption of sounds

substance abuse Excessive use of an addictive substance

unique Not usual or common

Find Out More

Books

Lajiness, Katie. *Ed Sheeran*. Minnesota, Minneapolis, MN: BIG BUDDY BOOKS, an Imprint of Abdo Publishing, 2017.

Morreale, Marie. *Ed Sheeran*. New York: Childrens Press, an Imprint of Scholastic Inc., 2015.

Nolan, David. *Ed Sheeran: A+ The Unauthorized Biography*. New York, NY: Lesser Gods, 2016.

Websites

Ed Sheeran Biography
www.biography.com/people/ed-sheeran

"10 facts about Ed Sheeran!"
www.funkidslive.com/blog/10-facts-about-ed-sheeran/

Index

About the Author

Rachel Seigel is an avid reader and book enthusiast. She has more than 15 years of experience writing books for children and adults for elementary school, high school, and public libraries. She is the author of several nonfiction books for children.